Contents — Violin Book Three

£7.99

Rocky mountain

American folk song

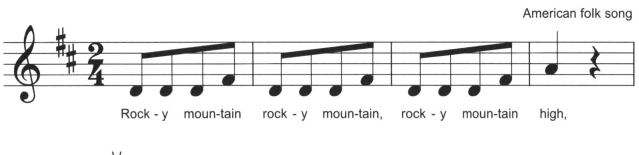

Rock - y moun-tain rock - y moun-tain, rock - y moun-tain high,

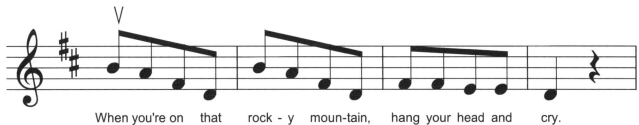

When you're on that rock - y moun-tain, hang your head and cry.

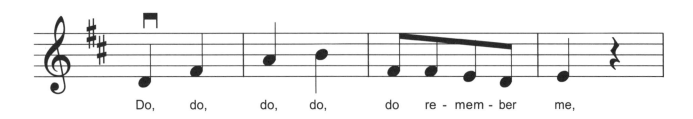

Do, do, do, do, do re - mem - ber me,

Do, do, do, do, do re - mem - ber me.

Russian folk song

Add your own dynamics to this tune.

London Bridge

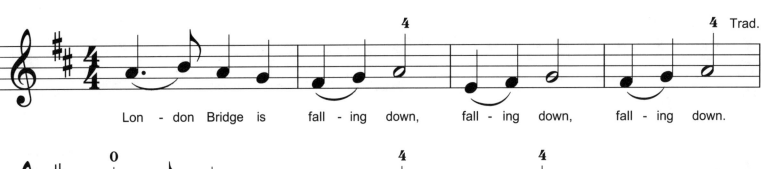

Lon - don Bridge is fall - ing down, fall - ing down, fall - ing down.

Lon - don Bridge is fall - ing down, my fair la - dy.

3

Minuet

Michel Corrette
(1709-1795)

Queen Mary

Trad. Scottish

Sailors' hornpipe

French folk song

6

Kookaburra

Trad. Australian round

Kook - a - bur - ra sits in the old gum tree,____ mer - ry, mer - ry king of the bush is he,____

Laugh, kook - a - bur - ra laugh, kook - a - bur - ra gay your life must be.

Steps and skips on E string

Oranges and lemons

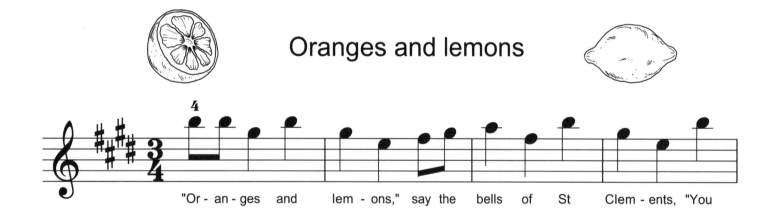

"Or - an - ges   and   lem - ons," say the   bells   of   St   Clem - ents, "You

owe   me   five   farth - ings," say the   bells   of   St   Mar - tins.

Shortnin' bread

Trad. American

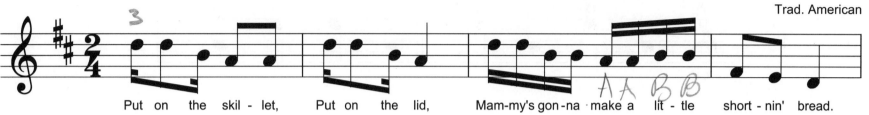

Put on the skil - let, Put on the lid, Mam-my's gon -na make a lit - tle short - nin' bread.

That ain't all she's gon - na do, Mam-my's gon - na make a lit - tle cof - fee too.

Mam-my's lit - tle ba - by loves short - nin', short - nin', Mam-my's lit - tle ba - by loves short - nin' bread.

Mam-my's lit - tle ba - by loves short - nin', short - nin', Mam-my's lit - tle ba - by loves short - nin' bread.

Fourth finger target practice

1

2

3

4

Hopak

Russian folk song

Ode to joy

Beethoven

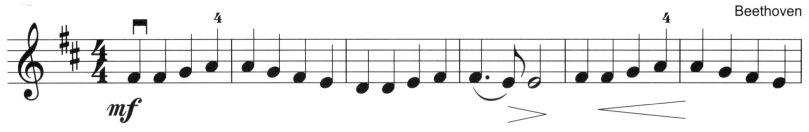

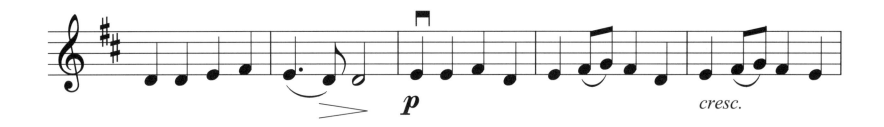

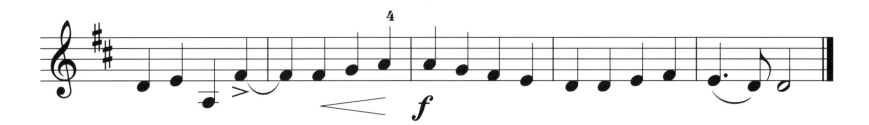

Michael Finnegan

Trad.

There was an old man called Mi-chael Fin-ne - gan, He grew whisk-ers on his chin - ne - gan, The

wind came up and blew them in a - gain, Poor old Mi - chael Fin - ne - gan, be - gin a - gain.

Staccato: short notes

Stop the bow between notes.

My hat

German folk song

My hat, it has three cor-ners, Three cor - ners has my hat. And

had it not three cor-ners, It would not be my hat!

J'ai du bon tabac

French folk song

$\overset{\bullet}{\rule{0pt}{1em}}$ = staccato = play short notes $\overset{\rule{0.7em}{0.1em}}{\rule{0pt}{1em}}$ = tenuto = play full value notes

G major study

Can you tell me?

German folk song

Étude

Czerny

Violin 1

Violin 2

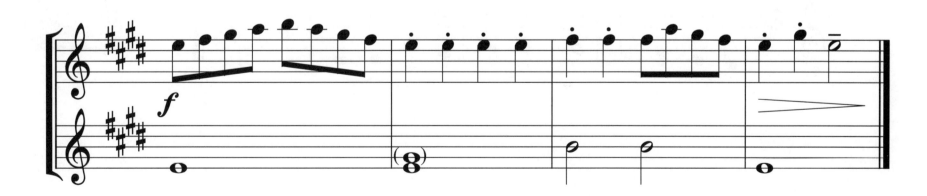

Mezzo staccato: short notes
Stop the bow between notes.

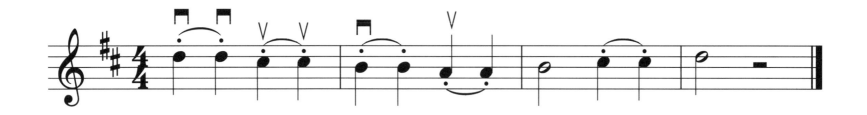

Merry dance

French folk song

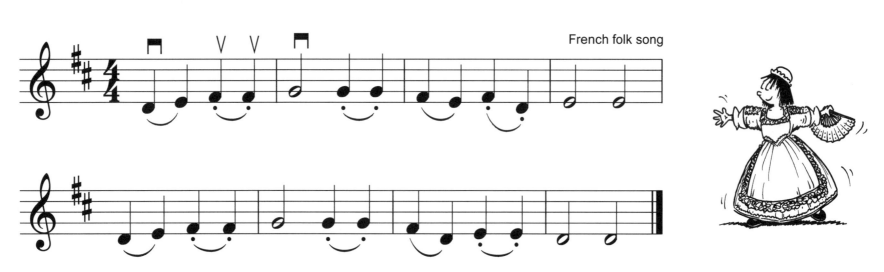

18

Second finger back next to first finger

D   E   F sharp   D   E   F natural

Melody

Rain, rain, go away

Rain,   rain,   go a - way,   come a - gain an – oth - er day.

High 2, low 2

1
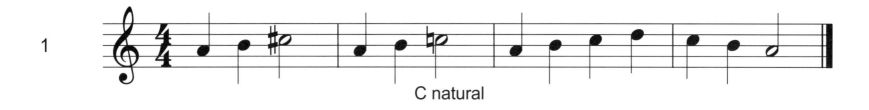
C natural

2

G natural

3
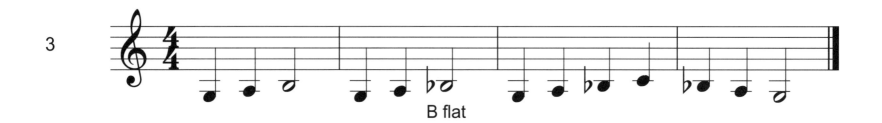
B flat

Burnt buns

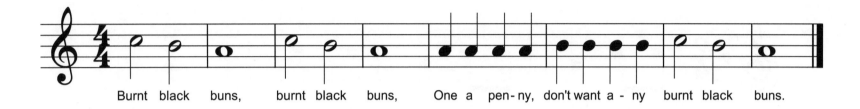

Burnt black buns, burnt black buns, One a pen-ny, don't want a-ny burnt black buns.

Sing high

Sing low

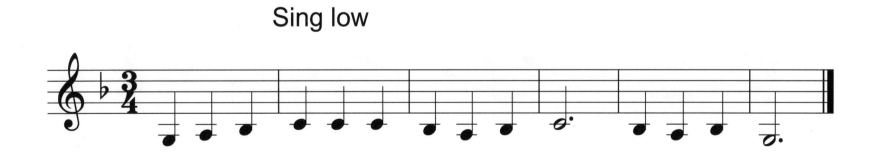

Teddy bear

Trad.

Ted - dy bear, ted - dy bear, turn a - round,

Ted - dy bear, ted - dy bear, touch the ground,

Ted - dy bear, ted - dy bear, show your shoe,

Ted - dy bear, ted - dy bear, that will do!

Playing in C major

This old man

Trad.

This old man, he played one, He played nick - nack on my drum;

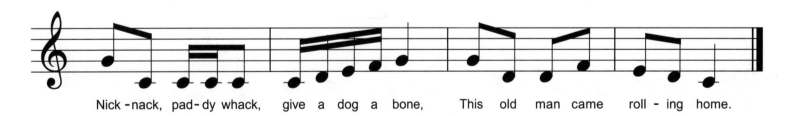

Nick -nack, pad- dy whack, give a dog a bone, This old man came roll - ing home.

I am a fine musician

I am a fine mus - i - cian, I prac - tise ev - ery day, And

peo - ple come from miles a - round, just to hear me play, My

vi - o - lin, my vi - o - lin, they love to hear my vi - o - lin, I

am a fine mus - i - cian, I prac - tise ev - ery day.

French folk song

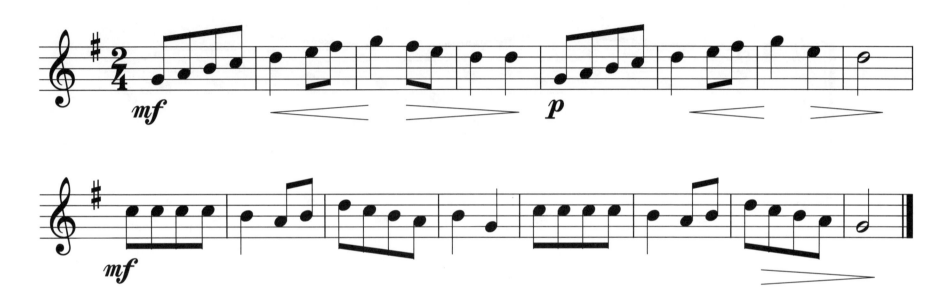

G major study

Yankee Doodle

Trad.

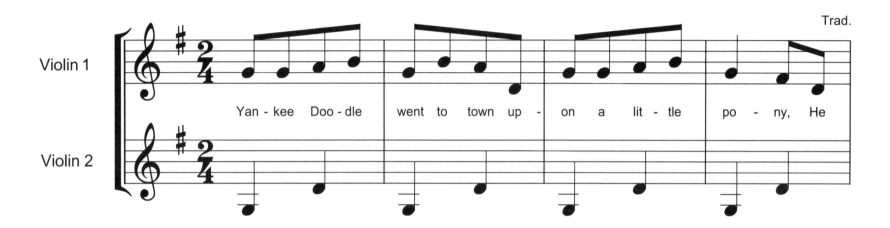

Violin 1 / **Violin 2**

Yan - kee Doo - dle went to town up - on a lit - tle po - ny, He

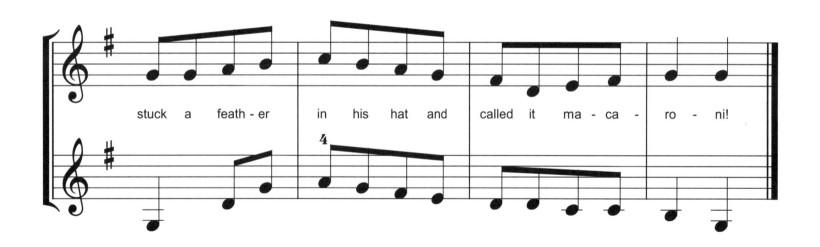

stuck a feath - er in his hat and called it ma - ca - ro - ni!

Happy birthday

Trad.

The grand old Duke of York

Trad.

Oh, the grand old Duke of York, He had ten thou-sand men, He marched them up to the top of the hill and he marched them down a - gain. And when they were up, they were up, and when they were down, they were down, And when they were on - ly half - way up, they were nei - ther up nor down.

28

She'll be comin' 'round the mountain

Trad.

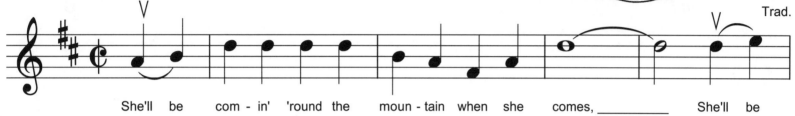

She'll   be   com - in' 'round the   moun - tain when she   comes, _____   She'll   be

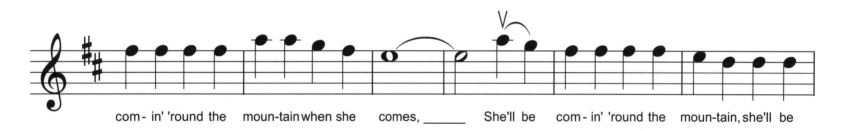

com - in' 'round the   moun-tain when she   comes, _____   She'll be   com - in' 'round the   moun-tain, she'll be

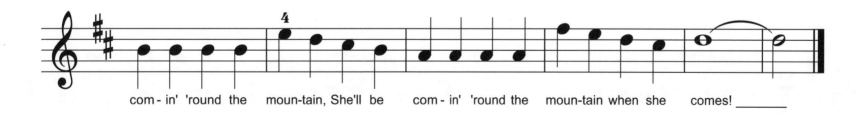

com - in' 'round the   moun-tain, She'll be   com - in' 'round the   moun-tain when she   comes! _____

Tallis' canon

Thomas Tallis
c. 1561

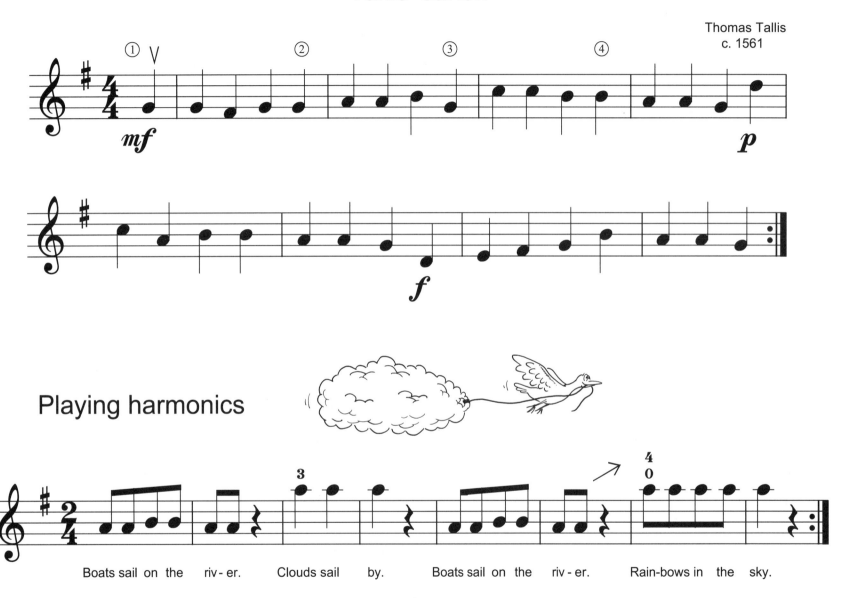

Playing harmonics

Boats sail on the riv - er. Clouds sail by. Boats sail on the riv - er. Rain-bows in the sky.

Fly around

Trad.

Fly a - round my pret-ty lit - tle miss, Fly a - round my dais - y,

Fly a - round my pret-ty lit - tle miss, You al - most drive me cra - zy,

Gon - na buy some weev-il - y wheat, Gon - na buy some bar - ley,

Gon - na buy some weev-il - y wheat, And bake a cake for Char - lie.

Tenuto: full value notes
Stop the bow between notes.

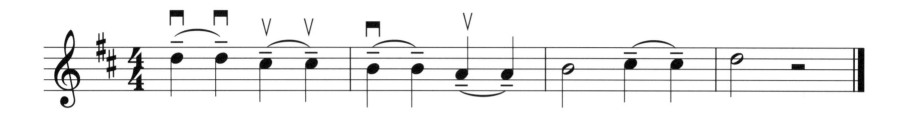

Russian folk song

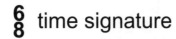 **time signature**

 = 1

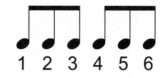

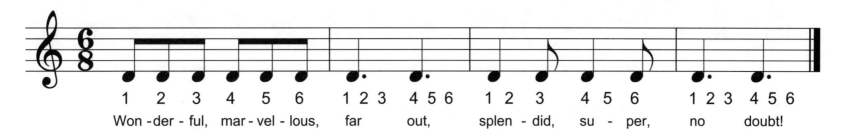

Won - der - ful, mar - vel - lous, far out, splen - did, su - per, no doubt!

Hickory, dickory, dock

Hick - or - y, dick - or - y, dock, The mouse__ ran up__ the clock. The

clock struck one, the mouse ran down, Hick - or - y, dick - or - y, dock!

33

It's raining, it's pouring

Trad.

It's rain - ing, it's pour - ing, the old man is snor - ing, He bumped his head on the foot of the bed and he could-n't get up till the morn - ing.

Row, row, row your boat

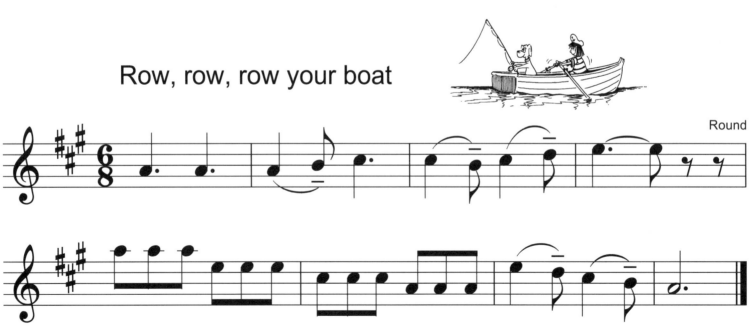

Round

Over the hills and far away

Trad.

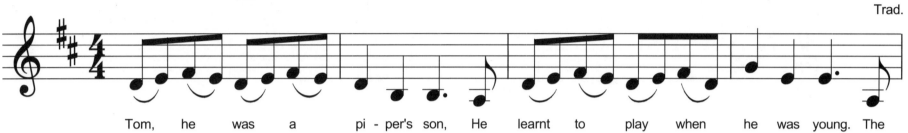

Tom, he was a pi - per's son, He learnt to play when he was young. The

on - ly tune that he could play, was 'O - ver the hills and far a - way'.

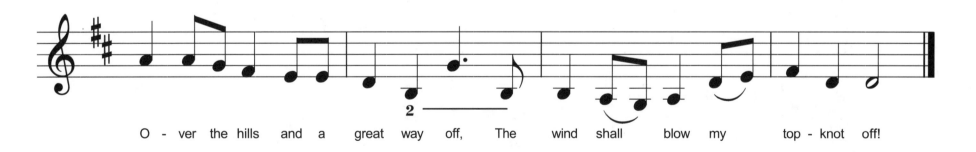

O - ver the hills and a great way off, The wind shall blow my top - knot off!

Three blind mice

Trad. round

The wraggle taggle gipsies, O!

Trad.

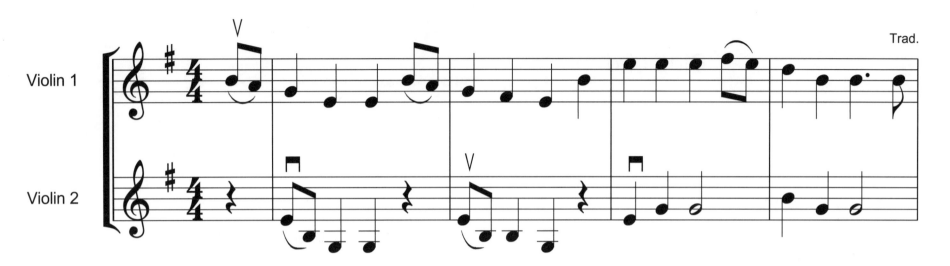

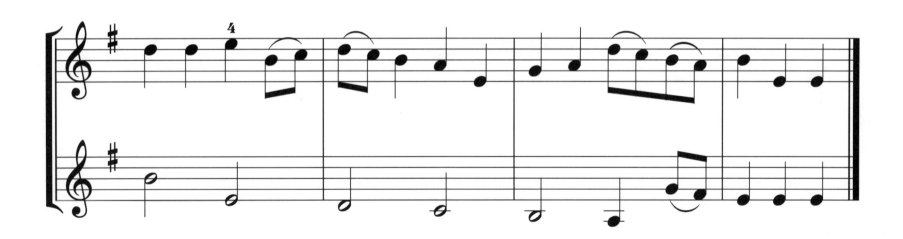

37

Blue bird

Trad.

Blue bird, blue bird, fly through my win - dow, Blue bird, blue bird, fly through my win - dow.

Blue bird, blue bird, fly through my win - dow, Fly a - way from here.

Norwegian dance

Trad.

Summer is a-coming in

13C round

Sum - mer is a - com - ing in _____, Loud - ly sing cuc - koo.

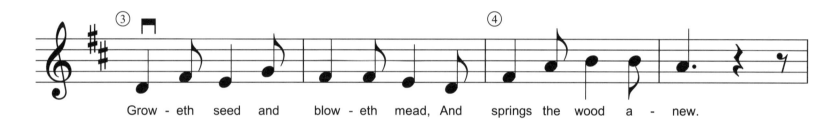

Grow - eth seed and blow - eth mead, And springs the wood a - new.

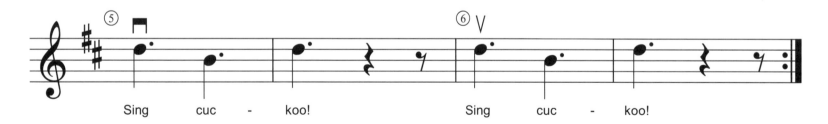

Sing cuc - koo! Sing cuc - koo!

Scarborough Fair

Trad.

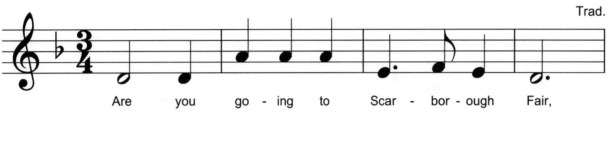

Are you go - ing to Scar - bor - ough Fair,

Par - sley, sage, rose - ma - ry and thyme; Re -

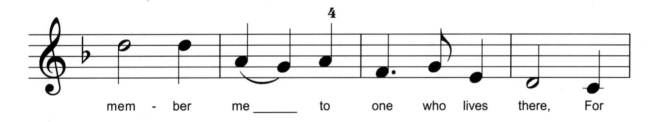

mem - ber me _____ to one who lives there, For

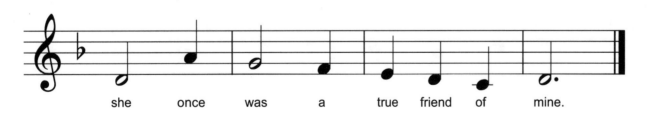

she once was a true friend of mine.

41

Dutch folk song

Hornpipe

Trad. Scandinavian

More harmonics

One for the mo - ney, two for the show, three to get read - y, GO MAN GO!

Ho-la-hi, ho-la-ho!

German folk song

44

Davy knick knack

Trad. Scottish

1. Play with separate bows (whole and half bows). **Scales and arpeggios**
2. Play with slurs (whole bows).

A major

D major

G major

G major

C major

Bowing variations (scale, arpeggio or melody)

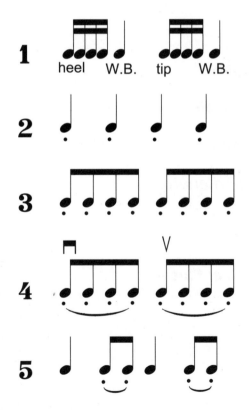

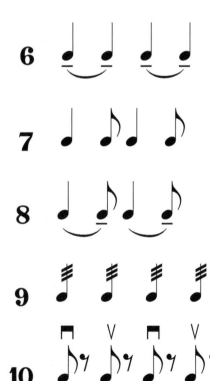

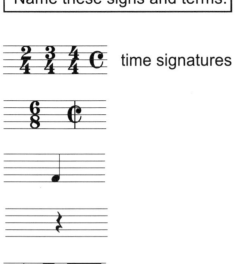 time signatures

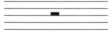

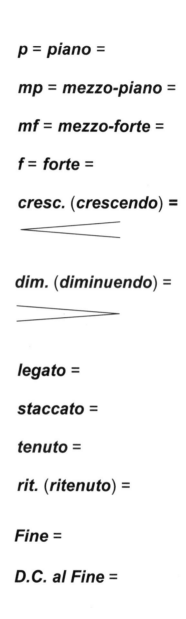

p = **piano** =

mp = **mezzo-piano** =

mf = **mezzo-forte** =

f = **forte** =

cresc. (**crescendo**) =

dim. (**diminuendo**) =

legato =

staccato =

tenuto =

rit. (**ritenuto**) =

Fine =

D.C. al Fine =